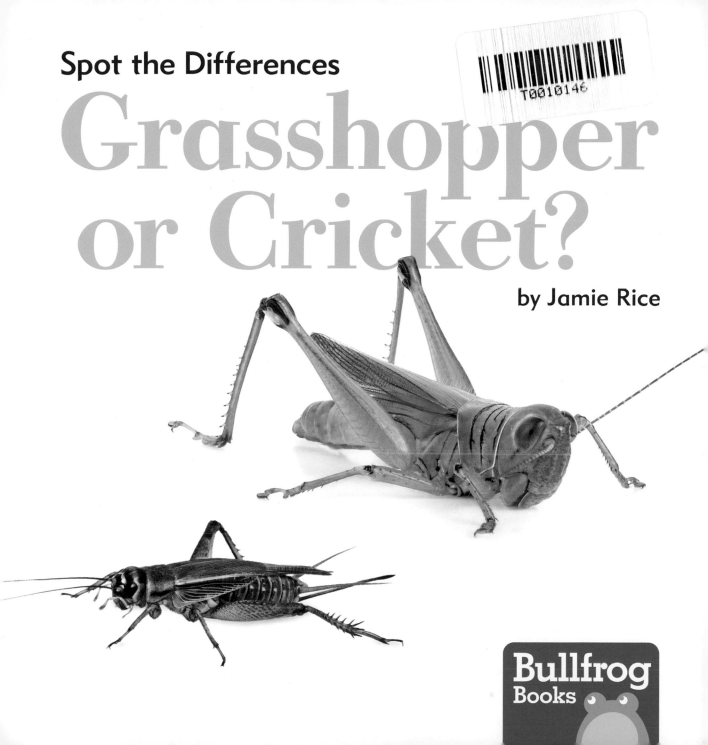

# Spot the Differences
# Grasshopper or Cricket?

by Jamie Rice

Bullfrog Books

# Ideas for Parents and Teachers

Bullfrog Books let children practice reading informational text at the earliest reading levels. Repetition, familiar words, and photo labels support early readers.

## Before Reading

- Discuss the cover photo. What does it tell them?

- Look at the picture glossary together. Read and discuss the words.

## Read the Book

- "Walk" through the book and look at the photos. Let the child ask questions. Point out the photo labels.

- Read the book to the child, or have him or her read independently.

## After Reading

- Prompt the child to think more. Ask: What did you know about grasshoppers and crickets before reading this book? What more would you like to learn?

Bullfrog Books are published by Jump!
5357 Penn Avenue South
Minneapolis, MN 55419
www.jumplibrary.com

Library of Congress Cataloging-in-Publication Data

Names: Rice, Jamie, author.
Title: Grasshopper or cricket? / by Jamie Rice.
Description: Minneapolis, MN: Jump!, Inc., 2023.
Series: Spot the differences | Includes index.
Audience: Ages 5–8
Identifiers: LCCN 2022011677 (print)
LCCN 2022011678 (ebook)
ISBN 9798885241649 (hardcover)
ISBN 9798885241656 (paperback)
ISBN 9798885241663 (ebook)
Subjects: LCSH: Grasshoppers—Juvenile literature.
Crickets—Juvenile literature.
Classification: LCC QL508.A2 R455 2023 (print)
LCC QL508.A2 (ebook) | DDC 595.7/26—dc23/eng/20220408
LC record available at https://lccn.loc.gov/2022011677
LC ebook record available at https://lccn.loc.gov/2022011678

Editor: Katie Chanez
Designer: Emma Bersie

Photo Credits: Vitalii Hulai/Shutterstock, cover (top); Mr. SUTTIPON YAKHAM/Shutterstock, cover (bottom), 1 (top); Evgeny Parushin/Shutterstock, 1 (bottom); SIMON SHIM/Shutterstock, 3, 16–17, 23br; Ksenia Lada/Shutterstock, 4, 23tr; Petr Ganaj/Shutterstock, 5; blickwinkel/Alamy, 6–7 (top); Sanjay M Dalvi/Shutterstock, 6–7 (bottom); Tyler Fox/Shutterstock, 8–9; Roberta Olenick/All Canada Photos/SuperStock, 10–11, 23bl; Ch'ien Lee/Minden Pictures/SuperStock, 12–13, 23tl; Avalon.red/Alamy, 14–15; Bryan Reynolds/Alamy, 18–19; Zuzha/Shutterstock, 20; Peter Waters/Shutterstock, 21; Alexander Sviridov/Shutterstock, 22 (left); Peter Yeeles/Shutterstock, 22 (right); Sapadia Aku/Shutterstock, 24 (top); chinahbzyg/Shutterstock, 24 (bottom).

Printed in the United States of America at Corporate Graphics in North Mankato, Minnesota.

# Table of Contents

A grasshopper hums.
How?
It rubs its legs on its wings.
A cricket chirps.
It rubs its wings together.
Which is this?

## How to Use This Book

In this book, you will see pictures of both grasshoppers and crickets. Can you tell which one is in each picture?

**Hint:** You can find the answers if you flip the book upside down!

# Green or Brown?

This is a grasshopper.

# This is a cricket.

Both are insects.

They look the same.

But they are not.

How?

Let's see!

A grasshopper is often green.

A cricket is often brown.

Which is this?

A grasshopper may have yellow, blue, or red marks.

A cricket does not.

Which is this?

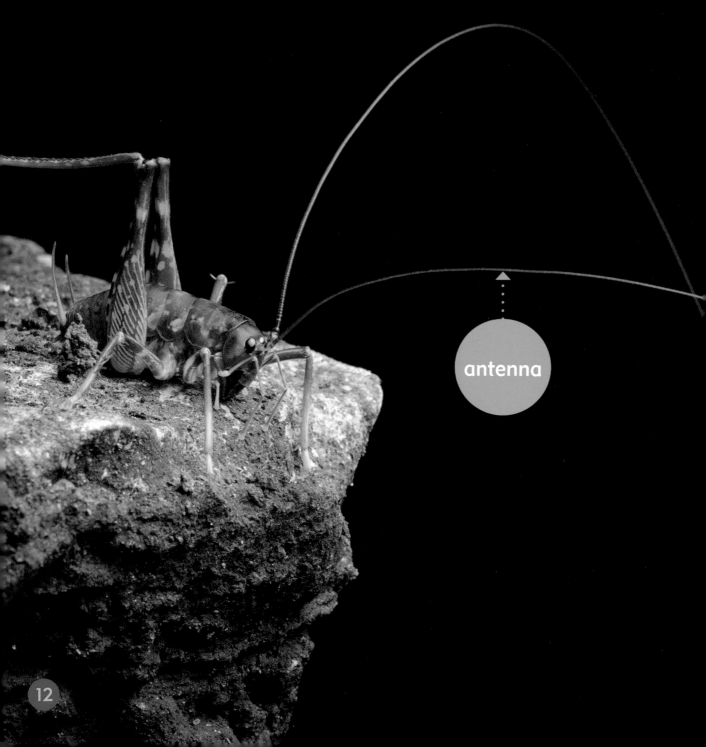

antenna

Each has two antennas.

A grasshopper's are short.

A cricket's can be longer than its body!

Which is this?

Both jump.

Long legs help.

A grasshopper jumps in the day.

A cricket jumps at night.

Which is this?

leg

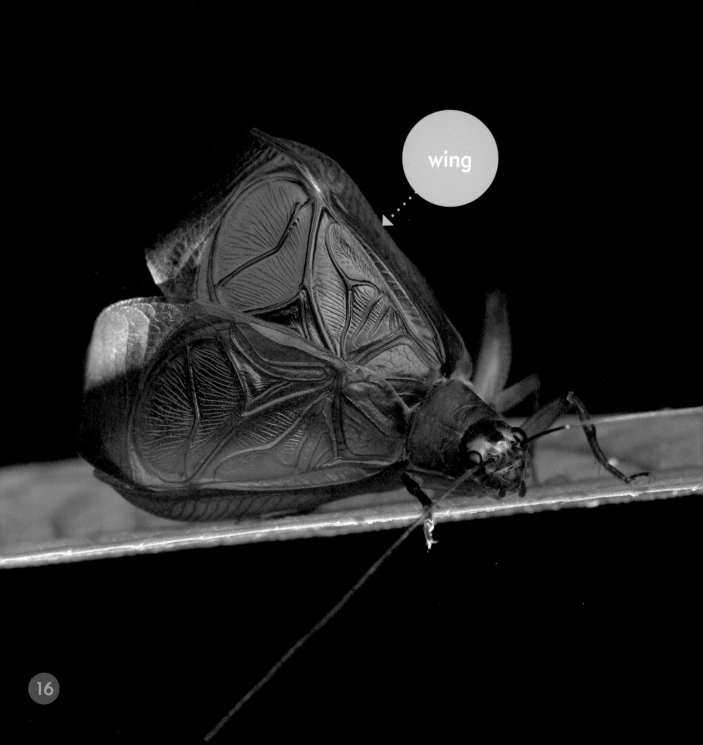

wing

A grasshopper hums.

How?

It rubs its legs on its wings.

A cricket chirps.

It rubs its wings together.

Which is this?

*Munch!*

Both eat plants.

A cricket eats insects, too.

Which is this?

# See and Compare

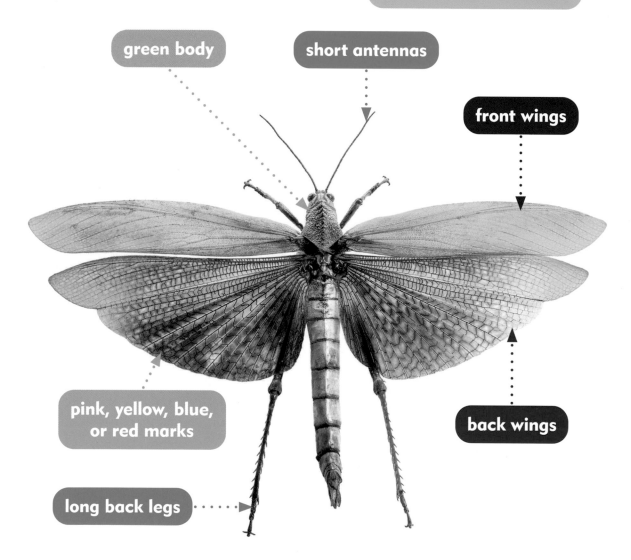

green body

short antennas

front wings

pink, yellow, blue, or red marks

back wings

long back legs

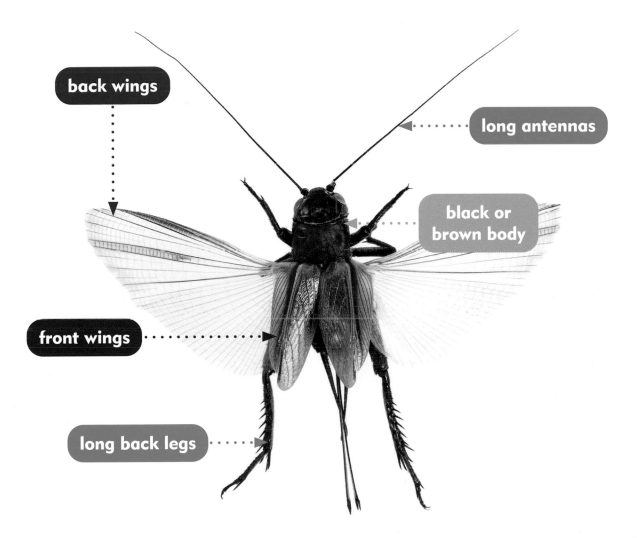

back wings

long antennas

black or
brown body

front wings

long back legs

# Quick Facts

Grasshoppers and crickets are insects. They have long back legs that help them jump. Two pairs of wings help them fly. They are similar, but they have differences. Take a look!

## Grasshoppers

- hum by rubbing their back legs against their wings
- only eat plants
- are most active during the day
- are often found in dry, grassy places
- can be more than four inches (10 centimeters) long

## Crickets

- chirp by rubbing their wings together
- eat plants and insects
- are most active at night
- are often found in damp, dark places, like under rocks or logs
- can be up to two inches (5.1 centimeters) long

# Picture Glossary

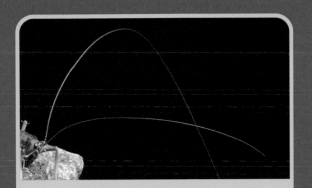

**antennas**
Feelers on the heads of insects.

**insects**
Small animals with three pairs of legs, one or two pairs of wings, and three main body parts.

**marks**
Small shapes or spots.

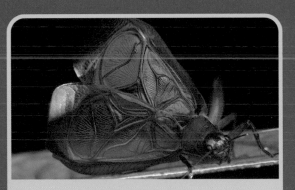

**wings**
Parts of some animals' bodies that they flap to fly.

# Index

# To Learn More

**Finding more information is as easy as 1, 2, 3.**

❶ Go to www.factsurfer.com

❷ Enter "grasshopperorcricket?" into the search box.

❸ Choose your book to see a list of websites.